Beware of the Modern World

Magic Quest, Volume 4

Gideon Crusader

Published by Gideon Crusader, 2022.

While every precaution has been taken in the preparation of this book, the publisher assumes no responsibility for errors or omissions, or for damages resulting from the use of the information contained herein.

BEWARE OF THE MODERN WORLD

First edition. November 17, 2022.

ISBN: 979-8201443283

Written by Gideon Crusader.

Also by Gideon Crusader

Magic Quest
A Codex on Creating a Magical Phantom
Prosperity Magic for Money & Wealth
Telekinesis Bible
Beware of the Modern World

Table of Contents

For J.

Introduction

Magic Quest: Beware of the Modern World is an occult and life manual that reveals the secrets and horrors of this world. As a magical practitioner, it is important that we become aware of the playing field that we are living in. The sad truth is that there are many evils in this world. Especially in this modern world, there are so many people who have been misdirected and deluded by the world. Be very careful because this world is deceiving, and it will not hesitate to destroy your soul.

Magic Quest: Beware of the Modern World will show you the evils that you should avoid, as well as how you can make the right adjustments in your life to free yourself from the many evils that corrupt this world. This is important since even as a magical practitioner, you are involved in this world, and you move in and out of this world. So long as you are alive, you must learn how to deal with this world in a way that will not make you forget who you really are.

This world, especially this modern world has been designed to make people forget who they really are and be like slaves. If you think that slavery is just a thing of the past, then you might want to reconsider your views. The truth is that slavery has just been modernized just as many things have also evolved in form, and yet not in substance. This is something that we have to deal with as magical practitioners.

I know many people who would like to spend more time with their spirituality but simply cannot do so because the world is keeping them very busy. This is a very common trap and yet its effects could be fatal to the soul. Indeed, we must be careful, and we should free ourselves from the many traps and evils of this world.

Know as early as now that this world is going to change who you are, and it will destroy you without mercy, especially if you are not aware of all the devious things that it is doing. Countless people have already fallen into its tasks without even realizing it. No wonder that according to official statistics, at least one person dies by suicide every 40 seconds. If this world is not sick enough, then how else should we view it?

The Modern World

It is true that modernization has brought about many good things; however, together with the good, evil things also came into the world. Back in history, when industrialization started, many artists and writers flew to far away lands, especially to areas rich in nature. They realized as early as then that the world was taking a different form, as well as a different form of evil.

As the modern world started to entertain the people with its so many material things, it also started to corrupt the soul of man. Right now, the state of things is such that if you are not living your life in accordance with the dictates of the modern world, then you might be mad. Interestingly, this kind of world has long been predicted by a number of saints and holy men and women of God.

How about you, where do you stand in this world? Are you able to see it as it truly is? Is your soul really alive and free?

The modern world has a structured form. Its system is very solid. Everyone who goes against this system or tries to escape it would have to face certain challenges. As a magical practitioner, you should overcome the evils of this world by going above them. The key lies in simplicity. By going back to how we used to be, back to our original roots and actually living it, we can make the change that the soul needs.

When a man is born into this world, they are already confronted by the system. As this human being grows, the more that they will be immersed into it until they are fully absorbed into the system, so much so that they will think and feel as the system wants them to do so. They will think and even believe that they are still acting on their own even though they are already being heavily manipulated. To realize that such evil has already taken place, one must be humble into nothingness. And, from this humility, one can finally find the way to be free.

BEWARE OF THE MODERN WORLD

- Why should we be careful dealing with the modern world?

- What is your current position right now in this world? Where do you stand?

- Know who you really are and never forget who you are.

On Humility

The first important step to realization of reality is to be humble. But what does humility mean? Humility is realizing our own nothingness. In the practice of magic which is, first and foremost, a spiritual practice, being humble is also very important. Without humility, divine graces cannot flow within us for we would be too full to accept anything new. As you read this book, it is kindly asked that you keep an open mind. You do not have to believe everything that you read, for you are encouraged to test every word and weigh their truth in your life. After all, the truth of one may not always be the truth for another. Nevertheless, we have taken the necessary efforts to present only the hard facts in this humble work, and it is asked that the reader may find the light in its darkness.

Humility compromises honesty knowing that we are nothing and that God alone is everything. If you are not a believer in the Divine, then that is okay. At least admit the fact that we, humans, do not know everything. In fact, some physicists go so far as to believe that the whole universe does not even exist. So, feel free to believe in whatever you want, but please keep an open mind.

There is a story in Buddhism that illustrates humility. The story goes something like this:

A novice monk visited a master monk. The novice monk wanted to impress the master so that he would take him as his disciple. So, the novice monk tried to impress the master by telling him everything that he knew. However, the master did not seem impressed and only sat there in silence. The novice monk soon kept quiet thinking that the master was not even interested in what he was saying. At that point, the master monk poured his tea into the cup. The novice monk watched in silence. Soon enough, he was surprised that the master kept pouring tea even though it was spilling already because the cup was already full. The novice monk felt very uncomfortable that he called the attention of the master to it, telling him to stop because the tea was already overflowing. But, the master continued to pour the tea. There was nothing left but silence and the sound of tea overflowing and getting wasted. At that point, the master finally stopped pouring his tea and asked the novice monk, "Do you see what happened here?" To which the novice monk replied, "I do not understand it." The master explained that just like the cup that could not receive new tea because it was too full of itself, so does the mind cannot receive new teachings when it is full of itself.

When we take the path of magic, we must approach it with humility of heart and mind. This is the first important step in the magical arts. When we are in this world, we must also maintain that humility at all times; otherwise, we could easily get lost in this world. In fact, many people who would be reading this book are already lost without even realizing it, for the majority of the people these days are caught in the illusions of this world. Indeed, this world is a shrewd one and so we must be careful.

Quick Review

- What does it mean to be humble?

- Why do we need to be humble?

On Slavery

Many people think that slavery is gone. But, is slavery really just a thing of the past or is it still present in our modern time?

The modern world has modernized many things, even slavery. If you think that slavery is just a thing of the past, then you might want to look around and reconsider your view. Slavery begins in school, where children are programmed to keep following the words of someone. The system of the world has also been programmed to make people trust it. These days, if you are not "educated" by a school, it seems that you are less than the others. Of course, in divine truth, that is simply not correct. But, the world has changed how people think and even feel toward many things. Still, as a magical practitioner, you must not allow yourself to be influenced by the world. We have to break free from all its traps and chains.

School is just the beginning where the mind is molded and prepared by the world to further accept its teachings. Still, it is a very important part of the "initiation" into the world. Now, after school, and assuming that the person has not realized the illusions of the world, the work environment comes next. Here, things will take a higher level as the person will most likely be introduced to the "real" importance and value of money. This is where the so-called rat race begins and the extreme competition among the workers and employees.

Assuming that the human being in our example applies himself to the usual course of life, he will soon be eligible to climb the ladder of employment. During this period, he will be putting into practice all the teachings on obedience and preparatory slavery that he has learned from school. This setup is not at all bad for it will reward those who will submit themselves to the system by increasing their income or some other form of compensation. This will only deepen the program in the mind of a worker, causing them to get even more trapped in the system of the world.

The labor and/or hours of work is also something that one must deal with carefully. Many of us end up spending so little time with our family and loved ones. These days, when a person is not busy enough, when they are not stressed out enough, it seems that they are not doing enough. Worse, a demon might even whisper, "You are not important." However, this should not be the case. One's worth must not be limited by the stress and pressures that they are dealing with. However, the system is geared and designed in such a way that one has to be always busy and always stressed to find meaning and self-worth. But, as a magical practitioner, know that this is not true, and you must not support this kind of lifestyle.

There are also many evils happening in the workplace. This is understandable since the minds of the people in such an environment have, usually, already been corrupted by the modern system. Indeed, we must be careful of how we live our lives.

Although many people are taught to pursue their dreams, a majority of the workers are employed in jobs that they have no passion in. This means that they are only there for the money.

BEWARE OF THE MODERN WORLD

It is all about the money in this world after all. However, the problem here is that many people are now performing certain jobs without passion, without love. They are unhappy and unsatisfied with their lives, hoping every day that something would happen that could change their life for the better. They are both trapped and enslaved by the system in which they have put their trust. The sad part here is that this same system in which they have trusted will not ever free them from its traps, but would even further enslave them, casting them deeper and deeper into the ways of the modern world, thereby making them forget who they really are and completely destroying their souls.

<u>*Quick Review*</u>

- Does slavery still exist in our present age?

- How does it begin and work these days?

On Competition

Competition is something that many people these days believe in. If you are not up for some competition, then perhaps you are simply not good enough, right? After all, competition also ensures that the market receives the best services. Indeed, it seems reasonable and well, but this same competition is actually one of the many causes of stress, anxiety, and hatred among the people.

Competition is the modern-day gladiator, except that, this time, the warriors do not need to battle with physical weapons. It is the modern age, and so it is now a higher form of war—the battle of the minds. This approach ensures having to destroy one another. Although it may be done indirectly as we need to keep things "professional", of course, nevertheless the spirit of destruction that is present in this kind of setup would remain and its adverse effects are the same.

Competition is good for those who make it. But, how about the majority that would be under the winners of this competition? Winning the competition necessarily involves placing the others below you. In this illusory world, this may please you for some time; but then, look at how it would affect everyone else? Look at the bigger picture and see its effects.

Instead of competition, one should work on building cooperation, teamwork, and a mutual sense of doing what is right and good. Instead of only one or two people going up leaving the others behind, let us build one another up. Together, as one team.

BEWARE OF THE MODERN WORLD

<u>Quick Review</u>

- What is competition?

- What are the evils that are inherent in competition?

Everything is Business

In the practice of magic, we always talk about magical energy, which is spiritual in nature. However, it must be realized that the energy in this gross material plane is now money. Hence, the modern world has been designed with a business approach in mind. Everything has a cost; everything requires you to spend some money. Again, it is all about the money. The truth is, money is just paper, and it is supposed to be abundant for everyone, but abundance for all is not the key to exercising power over the people. Hence, they keep the money limited but making sure that they own a bigger lot of it.

In business, just like the human blood, money has to be continuously moving/flowing. This is necessary to keep the business alive and functioning. But, what is the cost of running this business? In our world today, people have learned to see everything in terms of money. Sadly, even humans are now being weighed in terms of how much money they have in their wallet or bank accounts. Money has taken the key indicator on everything. However, as a magical practitioner, we know that this is not the right path, and we do not support it.

In this business setup, certain evils come into play. In order to increase production, businesses inject many chemicals on the animals that we end up consuming. According to studies, this is also one of the reasons behind certain serious diseases. Now, this will naturally lead to bad health for the consumers. Once health becomes compromised, hospitals will come into place, charging huge amounts of money for their service. Not only that, but the infamous pharmaceutical companies will also come into play, selling whatever medicines they have that are supposed to make you feel better and maintain your health. These days, the term "maintenance medicines" have become very common. But, what are we really maintaining when we make use of these medicines? Is it our health or is it to ensure that we are able to maintain the business of pharmaceutical companies? Various studies and experiments have been conducted showing that there are other modes and more natural means of healing without having to depend on maintenance medicines. Sadly, these modes of healing which used to be the main healing approach have now been coined as mere alternative medicines; and, only a few people are aware of how to use them properly and effectively.

We live in a time when most people are just mainly concerned about making money. As a magical practitioner, you must not be like them. Money does not define us. Businesses will make people think (and even feel) that their system is right, and that money is the most important thing in the world. Be very careful that you do not fall into such a worldly trap. There have been countless who have fallen into this trap; and because of that, they have lost their souls.

I am not saying that money is completely bad, but we must be cautious of our relationship with money. Business is also not always bad, but we must be careful that we do not cross the line and make us forget what is good and noble. Sadly, the system of the modern world has become so worse that it even makes profit at the expense of the lives of the people.

<u>*Quick Review*</u>

- What is the energy of this gross material/physical plane?

- Why should you be cautious of the businesses in this modern world?

- Is business always evil?

Living in the Future

Another very common trap as set by this world is to make people live in the future, not in the present moment. The modern system has a ladder, and it has prepared your life for you. Once you set out on a particular path, the system will handle the rest. And, as long as you are loyal to the system, it will soon reward you over time. Sadly, these rewards may not always happen; nevertheless, people still put their trust in the system, and rely on it. Many people these days would like to press the fast forward button so they could skip the present moment and just forward to a time when they would be in a much better situation.

Things were not like so in the Old Days, a time when man and nature were one. There was no future, for the present moment was already enough. People were living in the present moment, experiencing the joys and miracles of life. It was a time of magic, simplicity, peace, and love. Sadly, the modern system has made us forget all of this, and it makes people want to live in the future because the system promises a better life for the future. But, what happens to the present moment, the moment of *Now*? Unfortunately, many people these days are passing through life just waiting for the future. They fail to realize that the future is never certain, and that only the present moment is real. As a magical practitioner, we ought to exist and experience the present moment. Of course, this does not mean that we should not have plans for the future. We also have future plans, but we know and understand the fact that the future is not set in stone and is also uncertain. Because of this, we choose to live in the present moment, and we also choose to be happy in the present moment.

How about you, are you also living in the future instead of being fully present in the moment of now? In this regard, the practice of meditation is very much encouraged. Meditation takes us to the present moment and helps us to be aware. Sadly, many people are living their lives almost unconsciously, blind to the everyday miracles and wonders of creation and the universe. This is one of the significant differences between a layperson and a real magus.

A common sign that you are living in the future is when you keep thinking about the future. Again, this does not mean that you must not think about the future at all, but the future must not be the main thing that occupies your mind. Indeed, it is also good to have plans for the future as long as you do not get too absorbed into it that you could no longer get back to the present where you truly belong.

You must know and understand that only the present moment is real. You need to be present right here and right now. There is no other time, no other place to be. You must fully experience and enjoy this moment of now, and only then can you have a chance to be truly free.

<u>Quick Review</u>

- What does it mean to be living in the future?

- If not in the future, when where should you live?

- What is a common sign that you are living in the future and not in the present moment?

Meditation Practice

In all the practices of the magical arts, the practice of meditation is the one that is strongly encouraged. Meditation practice does not only bring us to the present moment, but it also naturally develops our overall psychic and magical faculties. It also deepens our spirituality. Indeed, if you are really serious about having any real progress in the magical and spiritual arts, then daily practice of meditation should be made a priority in your life.

Contrary to what many people think, the practice of meditation is actually very easy and simple. In fact, it is more about not doing anything rather than having to do something. Having said that, here is a basic and very effective meditation technique that you can start practicing right now:

Assume a comfortable position and relax. Close your eyes and do not think about anything. Breathe through your nose. With your eyes closed, gently focus on your breath. Breathe and let go of everything. If thoughts arise in the mind, which they normally do, simply ignore them. Keep your focus on the breath. Only the breath must exist in the mind. Be one with your breath and let go of everything else.

At any time that you want to end this meditation, simply bring your awareness back to your physical body. Once you can sense your body, slowly move your fingers and toes, and then very gently open your eyes.

BEWARE OF THE MODERN WORLD

Do not underestimate the power of this meditation. In fact, its power lies in its simplicity. It is a really effective meditation. Know that he who meditates on the breath, meditates on life. Be one with the breath (be one with life), be still, and let go.

It is not unusual for this meditation to take you into a state of mind that is peaceful and serene. It will also develop your overall magical faculties. Indeed, regular practice of this meditation will have significant effects on yourself. If nothing happens on your first several attempts, do not be discouraged. Just keep on practicing, and you will surely obtain good results in time.

According to the basic rules of magic and mysticism, one should meditate at least twice daily. If you can do more, then do so as it will be beneficial for you.

If you do some research, you will find that there are so many meditation techniques out there. However, you must know that you do not really need to learn all of these techniques. The reason for this is that all meditation techniques lead to one and the same path, and that is the path of spiritual enlightenment and magical development. The important thing is to actually engage in the practice of meditation, and that you must do it regularly.

With respect to the length of time that one is supposed to meditate, there are no strict rules on this matter. This is because once you reach a deep state of mind, time shall cease to exist. This explains how advanced meditators are able to sit in meditation for very long hours. This is something that comes about naturally by practice. For now, just focus on making meditation a part of your life. Practice it daily, and you will surely have positive experiences in time.

Quick Review

- Is meditation difficult?

- What are the natural benefits of meditation?

- How often should one meditate?

Dealing with Difficult People

As a magical practitioner, we must know how to deal with the various people around us. It is very easy to deal with those who are kind-hearted and loving; but the sad truth is that many people these days are obnoxious, egoistic, and rude.

The system of this world has corrupted the minds of so many people, thereby changing them. Sad to say, but the level of humanity these days is very low. Some would even think that it is already gone. In any case, we must not lose hope. The fact that there are people like you in this world means that everything is not yet completely lost. You are the hope that the world needs. Be yourself and never allow the evils of this world to change who you really are.

When it comes to dealing with difficult people you must learn to shield yourself, so that you will not be affected by their negative energies. Shielding is one of the basic magical skills. The technique that you are about to learn is a basic technique that is used even by advanced practitioners today. Its power lies in the skills of its caster. It is known as the *bubble shield*. It should also be noted that when we say that something is *basic* does not mean that it is weak; but rather, it means that it is important that you learn it. Having said that, the steps for creating a bubble shield is as follows:

Be comfortable and relax. Imagine a shield like a bubble around you. It may look like anything you want. It is suggested that you visualize it as a bubble of pure white light. Know that this energy bubble protects you from all negative energies.

The next step is to make this bubble shield strong enough to do its task. Imagine magical energy all around you. Feel free to visualize it in any way that you want. Again, seeing it as white light is recommended. Now, see and feel that you are drawing this energy toward you, and then pour that energy into your bubble shield, thereby making it stronger.

Keep adding energy into your shield to make it as strong and powerful as you can. You should be able to feel your shield getting stronger. Many times, I even see my shield lighting up with remarkable intensity of light. Continue this step for as long as you like.

Once you are satisfied with the power of your bubble shield, you can say an affirmation to further impress upon your shield its function. The magical affirmation can be as simple as saying to your shield, "You are my bubble shield, and you protect me from all harm and negative energies." Feel free to use a different statement if you wish. The important thing is to impress upon your shield its purpose.

It should be noted that psychic shields spend energy to continue to survive and do their functions effectively. On average, a shield that is created in the manner as aforesaid will last for about five hours. If you want to keep your bubble shield for a longer period, you will need to recharge it with energy before it disappears. Do not worry; this is very easy to do. Simply imagine your shield and magical energy all around you, and then pour energy into your shield again just as when you first created it. This will ensure that your shield has enough energy to continue to exist and perform its designated function.

If it ever happens that you could no longer feel your shield, simply feel free to make a new one. After all, it is safe to use this technique as often as you like. It is also a good practice to develop your skills in the fine art of energy manipulation.

Another benefit of using this technique is that once you get used to it, you can easily cast it at any time even in public, without anyone noticing that you are casting a defensive magic. It is recommended to practice this technique at least once daily. The more that you practice, the more effective your bubble shield is going to be. Always remember that practice makes perfect.

Although very helpful, casting a shield will not completely protect you from the many evils of this world. You should also make some adjustments in your life to free yourself from the traps and deceptions of the modern system. In this regard, having the right knowledge is important, which is also why this book is revealing to you the hard facts of this world.

Always stand your ground, especially during moments when the world is making you forget who you really are. Always stay kind and pure. Do not let the people take away your peace of mind. Remember that pain is physical while suffering is mental. You can free yourself from suffering by taking good care of your mind.

There will always be bad and rude people out there. Sadly, the modern world is so full of those kinds of people. But, do not lose hope, neither be dismayed. You do not have to turn yourself into the world. You can only be truly happy by being yourself. Embrace love and all positive energy, and keep yourself away from all negativity. Stay away from negative people. And, during those times when you cannot avoid being with them, be sure to keep yourself protected from their evil, and never allow them to be able to change who you are. Instead of allowing them to turn you into them, immerse yourself more into love. Love them and be kind to them. Who knows, your love might help them realize the darkness that they are in.

Quick Review

- What is the bubble shield and how do you cast it?

- How should you deal with difficult people?

On Losing the Soul

It is sad to say that so many people these days almost do not have their souls. They are lost without even realizing it. As a magical practitioner, you must take good care of your soul. Do not let anyone take it away from you.

It is very easy to lose one's soul in this world. The system is shrewdly designed to make one forget who they really are. Hence, in the practice of magic, there is what is known as *introspection*. Introspection is simply the practice of looking into one's self. Simply put, it is about getting to know yourself. It is encouraged that this should be made a daily habit. From time to time, stop to just watch yourself and get to know yourself. There are no hard rules on how to do this. The important thing is to spend some time alone and just examine yourself: the things that you do, your thoughts and feelings, your life in general and the specific things that are happening in it, how you spend your days and nights, and so on. The only rule here is to be very honest with yourself. The more honest and open you are, the better.

A common mistake in the practice of introspection is to keep a blind eye on one's weaknesses. Remember that you will benefit so much more from this practice if you pay attention to your weaknesses. In fact, it is more beneficial for you to learn from your weaknesses than from your strengths. Therefore, when you practice introspection, be sure to take note of both your strengths and weaknesses, with a special attention to your weaknesses.

Once you get to know yourself more, you should make sure that you are always yourself in your everyday life. Being yourself is not just a matter of mood, but it should be your state of mind and being all the time, even when you are exposed to other people.

If after self-examination you realize that you are one of the many who have gotten lost in this world, do not be disheartened. You cannot lose your soul completely as long as you are alive. So long as you are alive, there is hope for you. The important thing now is that you are aware, and that you can do something about it.

Knowing is different from actual change. Knowing is usually the first step. Making positive changes usually requires taking positive actions. The actions will depend on your personal circumstances. But, they all have the sam spirit — and that is gettin free from the bondage of the world and only being yourself.

Most people lose their souls through a long and gradual process. As we have discussed, it usually begins from a young age. It usually starts by influencing the mind. The key is to recognize these influences and start to think on your own. To assure that you get the right view, you must work on developing your spirituality. Take note that this is not about intellect, for many intellectual people are also under the spell of the world. The key lies in the soul. By elevating your soul through enriching your spiritual life, you can be free from the bondage of the world and be who you truly are.

When a person does not live by the soul but is driven by the pressures of the material world, the soul slowly suffocates; and then suddenly, life simply loses all its meaning. This probably explains why there are so many people these days who are committing suicide.

Be strong and of good courage. You have all the power within you to free yourself from the evils of this world. Find that power within and let it out. And, whenever you feel that you are simply not good enough, just remember this ancient wisdom: you are magic.

<u>*Quick Review*</u>

- How do we lose our soul?

- Do we completely lose our soul?

- What can we do to heal and regain our soul?

Slow Living

Slow living is getting popular these days. It should be clarified that slow living does not mean moving slowly; but rather, it means living with purpose and awareness. These days, so many people are going at a very fast pace, so much so that they could no longer stop to smell the roses — which is another way of saying that they could not even recognize and appreciate the beauty of life. They see it, but they can no longer realize its importance. They are too busy — too busy that they do not have the time to live.

It is good and healthy to practice slow living. You do not need to chase after the fast and unending rhythm of this world. It really helps to be more organized and to take things one at a time. Instead of always hurrying, live with more purpose and meaning. In fact, if you do things like this, you may be surprised just how much more you can accomplish with a more satisfying result. Not to mention, you will also enjoy a much desirable state of mind, even a serene peace of mind.

But how do you go about starting a slow living lifestyle? As usual, you shall begin with yourself. It is good to do some meditation before you plan out your daily tasks and your life. It helps to write down all the things that you usually do, as well as the things that you need to do. Now, here is the key: give more than enough time to accomplish every task or chore that you have. You must not hurry in doing anything. However, take note that you should spend all your time with quality. Slow living is not about being lazy and procrastinating. But rather, you should accomplish every work with peace of mind and with excellence, especially when excellence is necessary.

Slow living is something that you can do on your own by living more slowly, with more intention and purpose. You do not need to spend any money to start doing it, nor is there any requirement to be able to do it. Simply put, now that you know about it, it is all up to you whether you do it or not.

So, instead of scheduling 30 minutes to accomplish something, give it an hour. Apply this principle to all the other things that you must do, and you might be surprised just how this simple adjustment can have a huge impact on your life, as well as on your state of mind. From now on, you should never be in a rush to do anything. Be sure to take control over your time and the things that you do. Do not allow the pressures and stresses of this world to manipulate you. You can free yourself from the constraints of this world by rising above them. Yes, you can do this. You can be yourself right here, right now, and be free.

BEWARE OF THE MODERN WORLD

- What is slow living?

- How do you go about doing slow living?

- What are the benefits of living slowly?

- Does slow living mean literally moving slowly?

On Frugal Living

If one depends on money to be happy, then they will never attain true happiness because true happiness is never about money. It should also be clarified that being frugal does not mean being cheap. There is a big difference between the two. Being cheap is usually not good and displays a bad taste, but being frugal shows that you do not depend on money that much, and that you understand what money is truly worth.

I have to admit that back then, I was one of those who thought low about being frugal. I thought that it was just another word for someone who simply could not afford anything. But, the truth is, it is not really a sin or a problem to not be able to afford something. For, perhaps, you are too busy with something (or someone) that is much more meaningful and valuable than earning money. Money may be viewed as something of high importance by many, especially in this modern world, but we cannot erase the fact that money is still just a human invention and it has its limits.

The shrewd people may say that money is not the source of happiness, but money can buy the things that will make you happy. However, there is a problem with this seemingly cunning statement. We must be clear on what real happiness is. I am not saying that you will not be happy when you buy a new shirt or a new bag or whatever it is that is on your mind. However, is it the real happiness that your soul is seeking? Do you really believe that true happiness is all about buying material things? If one's true happiness is measured by the material objects that they buy, don't you think that it displays a much bigger problem? There might be something wrong with that person, isn't it?

Frugal living is not just about spending little money on things. In fact, the fact that you spend little money on things and stuff and the fact of being frugal itself is just a fruit of a deeper realization—and it is the realization that you do not depend on money for happiness. Hence, you now spend little on things because you see things and money just as they are—just mere objects, just as they truly are. Instead of being too attached to them, you would rather develop deeper bonds and share meaningful moments with your family and friends.

A good practice is to list down all the things that you love doing. Do they cost any money? If yes, how much? Moreover, are all these things really important to you? After doing this, list down the things that require you to spend money, such as for food and drinks, electricity, and so on. After doing this, find a way to lower your expenses, if possible. The key is to spend as little money as you can.

The more that we realize that we do not need that much money, the more that we can stop giving it so much importance. Instead, we can get busy with the truly important things in life, such as spending time with our loved ones, having quality time, pursuing our spiritual life, and so on.

As you can see, being frugal is not about being cheap, but it is a sign that we now understand the real worth and value of money—and that it is not as important as most people think it is. In fact, don't you think that it even looks really cheap if all someone cares about is money, especially if one's happiness is measured by money? Nothing could be cheaper than that.

Quick Review

- What does being frugal mean?

- Is money very important?

- Is being frugal the same as being cheap?

Do Not Believe the Mainstream Crap

Another very important lesson that we should know about the world is that it is heavily designed to manipulate people, such as how we think and even how we feel. We must not believe the mainstream news or everything that the world tells us right away. I am not saying that we cannot believe everything that they are saying, but it is important to also learn to always take their words and ideas with a grain of salt, and that we must think on our own. In many ways, the world is highly deceiving. The world wants us to trust the system almost without any question, as if everything that they tell us were true. Needless to say, many of the news and things being spread in this world are outright lies geared only to advance the interests of the world at the expense of the people.

Fortunately, these days, some people are already learning to think for themselves and question what those in authority tell them. Sadly, the majority of the population is still easily swayed by the world. As a magical practitioner, you must learn to stand your ground and think for yourself. A common trap of this world is that they combine truth with lies, just as they often combine good with evil. Unfortunately, in the end, the evil that they breed is much bigger than the good.

From now on, formulate your own view of the world, as well as what you believe in. This does not mean that you should be egoistic, but you should also keep an open mind. Still, it is good to have a clear understanding of your views so as to avoid getting easily swayed by the evils of this world. Again, be very careful for the world, indeed, is evil.

<u>*Quick Review*</u>

- Why shouldn't you believe the mainstream news and the stuff that you see online right away?

- What should you do to avoid getting easily swayed and manipulated by the world?

Best Practices

Let us now discuss the essential best practices that you can do to save yourself from the many evils of this world:

Meditate

The practice of meditation is definitely a must. It is a complete magical practice in and of itself. This also reminds me of the divine words as found in the Book of Psalms: "Be still and know that I am God." If you are serious about having any real and significant progress in the magical arts and in your spirituality, then it is a must that you prioritize your meditation practice, and that you must meditate as often as you can.

Live a simple life

It is strongly recommended to live a simple life. The modern world makes life very complex to the point that so many people are now stressed out and unhappy. Simplicity is key. Once you experience the beauty of a simple life, you will most probably not look back again. It should be clarified that a simple life does not mean a boring or a poor life. But rather, a simple life is a life that is filled only with what is important and essential to you.

There are no hard and fast rules on how you can simplify your life because it will usually depend on your personal circumstances. Still, the key here is to keep things simple and avoid having a busy schedule. Busy-ness is the thing of the modern world. In the past, when humans were living as real humans, life was simpler and people had more time in their hands to do what they really want, as well as to spend time with their loved ones.

Make friends with like-minded people

Another recommended thing to do is to form a bond of friendship with people who share the same passion and interests as you. Back then, I was able to make friends with a witch who was truly devoted to the practice of the Craft. I learned a lot from her, and we are very good friends to this day.

When it comes to choosing a friend, just be sure that the person is truly serious and passionate in pursuing the spiritual path; otherwise, it would be better to travel the path alone. Remember to work only with people who can help build you up, and not with those who would only discourage you from pursuing a genuine spiritual life.

Stay humble at all times

Humility is very important. When we are humble, we learn to become open. When we are truly open, divine energy will be able to flow through us. Humility makes us open to divine grace. And, as according to the words of the Divine Master: He who exalts himself will be humbled, and he who humbles himself will be exalted. Therefore, let us always be humble, so that the divine grace can enter us and lift us up, enlightening the soul.

Time for Solitude

In this very busy, modern world, a time for solitude is necessary. It is hard to think when we are exposed to a very noisy world. It would be easy to lose sight of who we are. Solitude is simply a time for peace and quiet on one's own. This should be a regular habit for magical practitioners, as well as for those who are seeking a deeper form of spirituality.

Enjoy the path

Regardless of the path that you are pursuing, enjoy it. After all, the magical path has no end. Happiness is also a choice. Even though we are exposed to this evil world, we can still decide to be happy. The world is not completely evil. There is hope. You are hope.

There is a battle between good and evil in this world, between light and darkness. Although darkness has been winning for so long now, it does not mean that the fight is already over.

Make time

Nobody will prioritize your magical and spiritual practices but yourself. Be sure to make time for your practices. This world has also been designed to make one forget about the spiritual life. The world will do its best to misdirect you and make you forget what is important. Be on your guard and be sure to examine yourself and your life every now and then, so that you will not stray away from the true divine path.

Know that you are not alone

The truth is that no matter where you are in this life, you are never alone. There are high powers out there watching over you. If ever you also have the gift of faith in your heart, you will surely understand more about this. But, for now, just know that you are not alone. You are never alone.

Quick Review

- Discuss at least three best practices that you should observe to protect you from the modern world.

- Why should you meditate?

- Why should you make time for your magical and spiritual life?

A Call to Christ

As some of my readers may already know, I am now a follower of Christ. I do not mean to offend whatever spiritual or religious ideas that you may have; but if there is any chance, I hope that you may give Christ a chance.

If ever you take this path, it is best to approach it with a clean slate — with perfect humility. You do not need to be a part of any religion to do this. In fact, religions tend to preach only the superficial part of the faith. Real faith comes by having a real relationship with Christ. It is also here where wonders and miracles unfold. If you study the lives of those who have followed Christ completely, you will see that their lives have changed a lot in a beautiful way, and they experienced so many miracles. In fact, most of the miracles of the saints would be considered of a very high magical level that even advanced practitioners could barely achieve. And yet, the only "credential" of such saints through whom the miracles happened is that they merely followed Christ. No occult knowledge or training of any kind at all. The miracles are diverse, such as miraculous healings even from terminal illness, resurrection of the dead, physical and spiritual protection, bi-location (being in two places at once), levitation, prophecy, communication with angels, and even the exorcism of demons, among many others.

There are also many witches and magical practitioners these days who are turning to Christ for a deeper and genuine spirituality. The problem with just pursuing a mere magical life is that after some time, magic becomes ordinary — and the soul will yearn for what is really essential, and that is the union of the soul with the Divine.

Again, do not let religion ruin your chance at getting to know who Jesus Christ really is. You can, on your own way, get to know Him. A good start is by reading the Bible. Do not worry, you do not need to read the whole Bible. You can start by reading the Book of Matthew, which also happens to be the first book of the New Testament in the Bible. It is not a long book, but you will learn about the life and divine teachings of Jesus — as well as how you can actually and directly follow Him.

Having said that, our humble journey ends here. I hope you have enjoyed reading this book. If you have time, please feel free to check out my other books. Last but not least, here is a word of wisdom from the Divine Master, and it is something that traditional ancient magic also supports: The kingdom of God is within you.

Quick Review

- How can we follow Christ?

- Where is the kingdom of God?

The Author

www.charlzdelacruz.com

Password to enter the private page: ANGEL912

Don't miss out!

Visit the website below and you can sign up to receive emails whenever Gideon Crusader publishes a new book. There's no charge and no obligation.

https://books2read.com/r/B-A-VRRV-SBXCC

BOOKS 2 READ

Connecting independent readers to independent writers.

Did you love *Beware of the Modern World*? Then you should
read *Telekinesis Bible*[1] by Gideon Crusader!

[2]

Magic Quest: Telekinesis Bible is a comprehensive occult manual
that discusses the magical art of telekinesis. What is telekinesis?
It is the magical art of moving objects with your mind. In any
practice of magic, your mind is your most powerful weapon.
By harnessing the powers of the mind, you can create wonders.
Telekinesis is not a new method. It has been in existence for
centuries. However, among the many seekers of this power, only
a few are truly able to learn it.

---

1. https://books2read.com/u/mqXoyZ

2. https://books2read.com/u/mqXoyZ

Magic Quest: Telekinesis Bible will not just teach you the theoretical part of telekinesis, but you will also learn its actual practices, so that you can try and see it for yourself. Interestingly, telekinesis is not really difficult to do. If you can devote enough time and effort, even by just practicing as little as an hour every day, then you can learn this ancient practice. It is also worth noting that telekinesis may be considered as a complete magical system in and of itself. As such, there are magical practitioners who focus solely on this practice alone. The reason for this is that there are other practices involved in the practice of telekinesis, especially if you truly embrace this craft sincerely.

Anyone can learn and do telekinesis -- yes, even you. Some people make the mistake of thinking that they could not learn telekinesis because they are not special or that they are not gifted. But, it must be clarified that you do not need to be special or be gifted with any extraordinary power to be able to do telekinesis. As long as you have a mind (which you have) and the power to imagine (which is also an inherent ability as a human being), then you can learn to do telekinesis.

Telekinesis is really an interesting and wonderful magical practice. However, do not think that it is all about just moving objects with the mind. Indeed, telekinesis is known for such a feat, but its practices can be diverse, which necessarily includes the practice of meditation and even the development of one's spiritual life.

Are you ready to embark on a magical journey that will have real and genuine manifestation to the point that it would affect physical objects? Are you ready to unleash the powers within you and move objects with your mind? If yes, then let me now welcome you into this magical universe of telekinesis.

Let us begin...

Also by Gideon Crusader

Magic Quest
A Codex on Creating a Magical Phantom
Prosperity Magic for Money & Wealth
Telekinesis Bible
Beware of the Modern World

www.ingramcontent.com/pod-product-compliance
Lightning Source LLC
Chambersburg PA
CBHW031126160726
47989CB00016B/1763